Earth Science

Study Guide

HOLT, RINEHART AND WINSTON

A Harcourt Education Company

Orlando • **Austin** • New York • San Diego • Toronto • London

ISBN 0-03-036346-2

5 6 054 08 07 06

Contents

Introduction to Earth Science 1

Earth as a System 3

Models of the Earth 5

Earth Chemistry 7

Minerals of Earth's Crust 9

Rocks 11

Resources and Energy 13

The Rock Record 15

A View of Earth's Past 17

Plate Tectonics 19

Deformation of the Crust 21

Earthquakes 23

Volcanoes 25

Weathering and Erosion 27

River Systems 29

Groundwater 31

Glaciers 33

Erosion by Wind and Waves 35

The Ocean Basins 37

Ocean Water 39

Movements of the Ocean 41

The Atmosphere 43

Water in the Atmosphere 45

Weather 47

Climate 49

Studying Space 51

Planets of the Solar System 53

Minor Bodies of the Solar System 55

The Sun 57

Stars, Galaxies, and the Universe 59

Skills Worksheet

Concept Review

In the space provided, write the letter of the description that best matches the term or phrase.

_____ 1. hypothesis

_____ 2. theory

_____ 3. geology

_____ 4. independent variable

_____ 5. dependent variable

_____ 6. astronomy

_____ 7. meteorology

_____ 8. oceanography

_____ 9. observation

_____ 10. peer review

a. process of obtaining information by using the senses

b. process by which experts in a field examine another expert's work prior to publication

c. scientific study of the oceans

d. explanation that is based on observations and that can be tested

e. factor that is manipulated in an experiment

f. scientific study of the universe

g. factor in an experiment that changes as a result of changes in other factors

h. scientific study of Earth's atmosphere

i. scientific study of the origin, history, and structure of Earth

j. explanation of a phenomenon based on observation, experimentation, and reasoning; supported by a large amount of evidence

In the space provided, write the letter of the answer choice that best completes each statement or best answers each question.

_____ 11. How does science differ from art, architecture, and philosophy?
  a. The goal of science is human endeavor.
  b. Science takes more mental energy.
  c. Science is the same as these other endeavors.
  d. The goal of science is to explain natural phenomena.

_____ 12. In their scientific study of Earth, what did the ancient Chinese do?
  a. record time
  b. keep accurate records of births and deaths
  c. keep records of earthquakes
  d. invent electricity

_____ **13.** What is Earth science?
  a. the scientific study of chemical mixtures
  b. the scientific study of Earth and the universe around it
  c. the scientific study of animal behavior
  d. the scientific study of life on Earth

_____ **14.** In the scientific process, forming a hypothesis is often immediately followed by what step?
  a. publishing the results in a scientific journal
  b. conducting a peer review of the hypothesis
  c. testing the hypothesis by conducting an experiment
  d. drawing conclusions about the hypothesis

_____ **15.** Which of the following is true about the impact of science on society?
  a. New technology created by science sometimes causes problems.
  b. The impact of science on society is always positive.
  c. Scientific knowledge does not help us understand our world.
  d. Science never has any impact on society.

_____ **16.** If experimental results do not support a hypothesis, what may happen?
  a. The hypothesis will become a theory.
  b. The hypothesis may be changed or discarded.
  c. The hypothesis will be published in a scientific journal.
  d. The scientist who developed it may resign his position.

_____ **17.** What area of Earth science is likely to involve the study of climate?
  a. geology
  b. biology
  c. astrology
  d. meteorology

_____ **18.** By tracking celestial movements, the ancient Maya were able to
  a. create accurate calendars.
  b. invent astrology.
  c. develop the scientific process.
  d. figure out geometry.

_____ **19.** What do scientists use to simulate conditions in the natural world?
  a. trial and error
  b. conceptual and physical models
  c. geology and meteorology
  d. books and records

_____ **20.** Scientific measurement is based on
  a. precision and accuracy.
  b. climate and weather conditions.
  c. independent and dependent variables.
  d. trial and error.

Name _____ Class _____ Date _____

Concept Review

MATCHING

In the space provided, write the letter of the definition that best matches the term or phrase.

_____ 1. asthenosphere

_____ 2. atmosphere

_____ 3. lithosphere

_____ 4. system

_____ 5. core

_____ 6. hydrosphere

_____ 7. biosphere

_____ 8. mantle

_____ 9. crust

_____ 10. geosphere

a. the solid, outer layer of Earth that consists of the crust and the rigid upper part of the mantle

b. the solid, plastic layer of the mantle beneath the lithosphere; made of mantle rock that flows very slowly, which allows tectonic plates to move on top of it

c. the thin and solid outermost layer of Earth above the mantle

d. the central part of Earth below the mantle

e. a mixture of gases that surrounds a planet or moon

f. the part of Earth where life exists; includes all of the living organisms on Earth

g. the layer of rock between Earth's crust and core; denser than the crust

h. the portion of Earth that is water

i. the mostly solid, rocky part of Earth; extends from the center of the core to the surface of the crust

j. a set of particles or interacting components considered to be a distinct physical entity for the purpose of study

MULTIPLE CHOICE

In the space provided, write the letter of the answer choice that best completes each statement or best answers each question.

_____ 11. The "middle sphere," the strong, lower part of the mantle between the asthenosphere and the outer core is called the
   a. biosphere.
   b. mesosphere.
   c. geosphere.
   d. atmosphere.

_____ 12. A system in which both energy and matter are exchanged with the surroundings is called a(n)
   a. open system.
   b. life system.
   c. closed system.
   d. free system.

_____ **13.** All of the following are processes through which Earth's energy and matter passes EXCEPT the

    a. phosphorus cycle.   **c.** oxygen cycle.

    b. nitrogen cycle.   **d.** carbon cycle.

_____ **14.** What are the Earth's pole-to-pole circumference and equatorial circumference measurements?

    a. 4,000 km, 40,700 km   **c.** 70,000 km, 40,700 km

    b. 7,000 km, 7,4000 km   **d.** 40,007 km, 40,074 km

_____ **15.** The force of attraction between any two objects depends on the masses of the objects and the distance between them, according to

    a. the law of magnetism.   **c.** the law of the magnetosphere.

    b. Newton's law of gravitation.   **d.** the law of plasticity.

_____ **16.** Earth's shape is a(n)

    a. oblate sphereoid.   **c.** perfect circle.

    b. oval.   **d.** circular spheroid.

_____ **17.** A community of organisms and their abiotic environment is called a(n)

    a. ecological system.   **c.** biological system.

    b. life cycle.   **d.** ecosystem.

_____ **18.** The possible source of Earth's magnetic core is

    a. Earth's ionized atmosphere.   **c.** the liquid iron in its outer core.

    b. the movement of the tides.   **d.** friction created by rotation.

_____ **19.** What can happen to energy as it passes through an ecosystem?

    a. It can be lost.   **c.** It can increase.

    b. It can be unchanged.   **d.** It can change form.

_____ **20.** Which factors do NOT control the balance of an ecosystem?

    a. producers   **c.** decomposers

    b. consumers   **d.** creators

Name _____ Class _____ Date _____

Concept Review

In the space provided, write the letter of the description that best matches the term or phrase.

_____ 1. elevation

_____ 2. latitude

_____ 3. conic projection

_____ 4. magnetic declination

_____ 5. longitude

_____ 6. topography

_____ 7. legend

_____ 8. cylindrical projection

_____ 9. azimuthal projection

_____ 10. scale

a. angular distance east or west from the prime meridian

b. size and shape of the land surface features of a region including relief

c. used to plot great circle routes used in air travel

d. angular distance north or south of the equator

e. angle between the direction of the geographic pole and the direction a magnetic compass needle points

f. height of land above sea level

g. used to produce a series of adjoining maps to make one continuous map

h. accurate near the equator, but distorted near the poles; parallels and meridians form a grid

i. the relationship between the distance shown on a map and the actual distance

j. a list of map symbols and their meanings

In the space provided, write the letter of the term or phrase that best completes each statement or best answers each question.

_____ 11. What are two ways scientists get data to make maps?
   a. field surveys and remote control
   b. word of mouth and legend
   c. field surveys and remote sensing
   d. books and the internet

_____ 12. Soil maps are used to
   a. show natural features and constructed features.
   b. show direction of the flow of groundwater and identify locations for waste disposal sites.
   c. record and predict weather events and plot precipitation.
   d. identify ways to conserve soil and plan sites for future development.

Name _____ Class _____ Date _____

| Concept Review *continued*

_____ **13.** A magnetic compass indicates direction because
      a. Earth has magnetic properties.
      b. geographic and geomagnetic directions are the same.
      c. everyone agrees which direction is north.
      d. a bar-shaped magnet is buried at Earth's center.

_____ **14.** What types of information do geologic maps show?
      a. distribution of climatologic features
      b. distribution of geographic features
      c. distribution of geologic features
      d. distribution of topographic features

_____ **15.** Each degree of latitude consists of
      a. 60 angles.
      b. 60 hours.
      c. 60 seconds.
      d. 60 minutes.

_____ **16.** What is a compass rose?
      a. a symbol indicating the 0° meridian
      b. a symbol that indicates the cardinal directions
      c. a symbol that shows the relationship of map distance to real distance
      d. a symbolic decoration

_____ **17.** any circle running east and west around the earth, parallel to the equator is a
      a. north-south circle.
      b. meridian.
      c. parallel.
      d. line of longitude.

_____ **18.** A geologic unit is a(n)
      a. amount of rock that fills a specific space.
      b. area that covers a quadrant on a map.
      c. volume of rock of the same type and age range.
      d. single rock.

_____ **19.** What is the only line of latitude that is a great circle?
      a. the prime meridian
      b. the equator
      c. 60°N latitude
      d. the arctic circle

_____ **20.** On a map, a contour line is
      a. a line that connects points of equal elevation.
      b. a line that surrounds a geographic point.
      c. a line between two points on the equator.
      d. a line that is the longest distance between two points.

Name _____ Class _____ Date _____

Concept Review

In the space provided, write the letter of the description that best matches the term or phrase.

_____ 1. chemical properties

_____ 2. ion

_____ 3. isotope

_____ 4. neutron

_____ 5. electron

_____ 6. atomic mass unit (amu)

_____ 7. physical properties

_____ 8. atomic number

_____ 9. proton

_____ 10. mass number

a. the number of protons in the nucleus of an atom

b. the sum of the number of protons and neutrons in an atom

c. subatomic particle that has a positive charge

d. unit of measure for the mass of subatomic particles

e. atom or molecule that has a negative or positive charge

f. characteristics that describe how a substance reacts with other substances to make new substances

g. characteristics that can be observed without changing the substance

h. subatomic particle that has no charge, located in the nucleus

i. subatomic particle that has a negative charge

j. atom with the same number of protons but a different number of neutrons as other atoms of the same element

In the space provided, write the letter of the answer choice that best completes each statement or best answers each question.

_____ 11. What is one way elements in the periodic table are arranged?
   a. in numerical order, heaviest first
   b. in alphabetical order
   c. in order of atomic number
   d. in order of number of neutrons

_____ 12. What are the three major types of subatomic particles?
   a. proton, neutron, electron
   b. nucleus, proton, byte
   c. quark, neutron, protron
   d. positron, neuron, electron

_____ **13.** What is true of elements in the same column on the periodic table?
  a. They have different arrangements of electrons.
  b. They have similar arrangements of electrons.
  c. They have similar arrangements of neutrons.
  d. They have different arrangements of neutrons.

_____ **14.** What is a compound?
  a. a substance made of physically bound atoms of two or more different elements
  b. a substance made of chemically bound atoms of two or more different elements
  c. any substance made of subatomic particles fused together
  d. two or more elements magnetically bound

_____ **15.** How do atoms form chemical bonds?
  a. by sharing or transferring electrons
  b. by mixing chemical solutions
  c. by sharing or transferring neutrons
  d. through magnetism

_____ **16.** What is an alloy?
  a. a solution of nonmetals
  b. metals melted together
  c. a heterogeneous mixture
  d. a solution of two or more metals

_____ **17.** What does the subscript mean in the chemical formula CO_2?
  a. two atoms of carbon
  b. two protons
  c. two atoms of carbon dioxide
  d. two atoms of oxygen

_____ **18.** What is the smallest unit of an element that keeps all of the chemical properties of a substance?
  a. atom   **c.** molecule
  b. proton   **d.** compound

_____ **19.** What is true of an atom with 8 valence electrons?
  a. It is reactive.
  b. It is missing some electrons.
  c. It is stable.
  d. It has more electrons than it needs.

_____ **20.** What is a mixture?
  a. a solution
  b. two or more substances not chemically combined
  c. two or more substances chemically combined
  d. a compound

Name _____ Class _____ Date _____

Concept Review

In the space provided, write the letter of the definition that best matches the term or phrase.

_____ 1. fracture

_____ 2. streak

_____ 3. radioactivity

_____ 4. density

_____ 5. magnetism

_____ 6. chatoyancy

_____ 7. cleavage

_____ 8. fluorescence

_____ 9. luster

_____ 10. asterism

a. the way in which a mineral reflects light

b. the tendency of a mineral to form smooth, flat surfaces along breaks

c. the ability of a mineral to glow under ultraviolet light

d. the color of a mineral in powdered form

e. the way in which a mineral breaks along irregular or curved surfaces

f. the cat's eye effect in minerals

g. the ratio of mass to volume in a substance

h. the appearance of a six-sided star shape when a mineral reflects light

i. the decay of a mineral's unstable atomic nuclei over time

j. the ability of a mineral to attract iron

In the space provided, write the letter of the answer choice that best completes each statement or best answers each question.

_____ 11. Which of the following describes silicate crystalline structures?
   a. single-sheet, cubic, prisms
   b. double-chain, hexagonal, tetrahedron
   c. sheet, isolated, ring
   d. cubic, hexagonal prisms, irregular

_____ 12. A framework silicate is one in which
   a. each tetrahedron is bonded to four others.
   b. each tetrahedron is bonded to two others.
   c. four tetrahedra are bonded to four others.
   d. each tetrahedron is bonded to six others.

_____ 13. A mineral is a natural, inorganic solid that has characteristic chemical composition,
   a. an orderly internal structure, and characteristic physical properties.
   b. silicate structure, and consistent chemical properties.
   c. nonsilicate structure, and consistent physical properties.
   d. a disorderly internal structure, and unidentifiable physical properties.

_____ **14.** Color is unreliable for identifying minerals because
   a. most minerals have similar colors.
   b. small amounts of other elements affect color, but weathered surfaces will reveal color.
   c. small amounts of other elements affect color, and weathered surfaces may hide color.
   d. most minerals are virtually colorless.

_____ **15.** What is the ability of a mineral to resist scratching called?
   a. asterism
   b. streak
   c. density
   d. hardness

_____ **16.** A silicate mineral contains a combination of
   a. silicon and carbon.
   b. silicon and oxygen.
   c. hardness and density.
   d. silicon and sulfates.

_____ **17.** A nonsilicate mineral is one that does not contain compounds of
   a. sulfates and sulfides.
   b. oxygen.
   c. sodium or calcium.
   d. silicon and oxygen.

_____ **18.** What is true of single-chain, double-chain, and framework arrangements?
   a. They are all types of silicate crystalline structures.
   b. They are all types of nonsilicate crystalline structures.
   c. They are not types of silicate crystalline structures.
   d. They are all unstable nuclei structures.

_____ **19.** Which are common nonsilicate crystalline structures?
   a. cubes, hexagonal prisms, irregular masses
   b. sheets, isolated tetrahedra, rings
   c. single-chains, hexagonal prisms, rings
   d. rings, chains, links

_____ **20.** What is true of the ions at the center of nonsilicate tetrahedra?
   a. They are oxygen ions.
   b. They are not silicon ions.
   c. They are silicon ions.
   d. They are carbon ions.

Skills Worksheet

Concept Review

In the space provided, write the letter of the definition that best matches the term or phrase.

_____ **1.** clastic sedimentary rock

_____ **2.** Bowen's reaction series

_____ **3.** intrusive igneous rock

_____ **4.** chemical sedimentary rock

_____ **5.** extrusive igneous rock

_____ **6.** cementation

_____ **7.** organic sedimentary rock

_____ **8.** compaction

_____ **9.** metamorphism

_____ **10.** rock cycle

a. the process in which one type of rock changes into metamorphic rock because of chemical processes or changes in temperature and pressure

b. rock that forms from the cooling and solidification of lava at Earth's surface

c. the simplified pattern that illustrates the order in which minerals crystallize from cooling magma according to their chemical composition and melting point

d. rock that forms when minerals precipitate from a solution or settle from a suspension

e. rock that forms when rock fragments are compacted or cemented together

f. the process in which the volume and porosity of a sediment is decreased by the weight of overlying sediments as a result of burial beneath other sediments

g. rock formed from the cooling and solidification of magma beneath Earth's surface

h. the process in which minerals precipitate into pore spaces between sediment grains and bind sediments together to form rock

i. the series of processes in which rock forms and changes by geological processes

j. rock that forms from the remains of animals or plants

In the space provided, write the letter of the answer choice that best completes each statement or best answers each question.

_____ **11.** Which of the following rocks is foliated?
  a. marble
  b. quartzite
  c. gneiss
  d. obsidian

_____ 12. Which of the following is NOT one of the three major types of rocks?
  a. sedimentary: formed from compressed sediment deposits
  b. igneous: formed from cooled magma
  c. obsidian: formed from rock that has small crystals; like glass
  d. metamorphic: formed when existing rock is altered

_____ 13. Which of the following does NOT affect the stability of rocks?
  a. chemical bonds between atoms in the minerals
  b. zones of weakness
  c. chemical and physical weathering
  d. the intensity of color

_____ 14. Which of the following is NOT an igneous rock texture?
  a. fine-grained   **c.** felsic
  b. vesicular   **d.** coarse-grained

_____ 15. Which of the following factors does NOT affect how rock melts?
  a. light
  b. pressure
  c. temperature
  d. presence of fluids in rock

_____ 16. What causes rock to change in regional metamorphism?
  a. Rock changes result from changes in temperature and pressure.
  b. Rock changes result from contact with nonfoliated rock.
  c. Rock remains unchanged after regional metamorphism occurs.
  d. Rock changes result from contact with magma.

_____ 17. The process by which different minerals in rock melt at different times
  is called
  a. compositional melting.
  b. partial melting.
  c. Bowen's reaction series
  d. metamorphism.

_____ 18. A common zone of weakness in rocks is called
  a. weathering.   **c.** a joint.
  b. composition.   **d.** a chemical bond.

_____ 19. Magma or igneous rock that is rich in feldspar and silica is
  a. porphyritic.   **c.** glassy.
  b. felsic.   **d.** mafic.

_____ 20. Which of the following is NOT a feature of sedimentary rock?
  a. stratification
  b. fossils
  c. cross-beds
  d. marble

Name _____ Class _____ Date _____

Concept Review

In the space provided, write the letter of the description that best matches the term or phrase.

_____ **1.** biomass

_____ **2.** ore

_____ **3.** geothermal energy

_____ **4.** solar collector

_____ **5.** fossil fuel

_____ **6.** hydroelectric energy

_____ **7.** anthracite

_____ **8.** permeable rock

_____ **9.** nodule

_____ **10.** petroleum

a. has interconnected spaces through which liquids can flow

b. is used in an active solar system

c. comes from organic matter such as plant material and paper waste

d. contains minerals that can be removed from it profitably

e. is produced by heat within Earth

f. can be found on the deep-ocean floor

g. is made of liquid hydrocarbons

h. is the hardest form of coal

i. is produced by running water

j. was formed from the remains of living organisms

In the space provided, write the letter of the answer choice that best completes each statement or best answers each question.

_____ **11.** The process that produces coal deposits is
   a. nuclear fission.
   b. placer mining.
   c. carbonization.
   d. contact metamorphism.

_____ **12.** What is the process by which the nucleus of a heavy atom splits, releasing neutrons and energy?
   a. nuclear fusion
   b. solar energy
   c. electrical generation
   d. nuclear fission

_____ **13.** Hydrothermal solutions moving through small cracks in rock may create
   a. ore deposits.
   b. placer deposits.
   c. nodules.
   d. lignite.

_____ **14.** A process that lessens the negative effects of mining on the environment is
   a. contact metamorphism.
   b. reclamation.
   c. surface mining.
   d. carbonization.

_____ **15.** An example of a valuable nonmetallic mineral is
   a. ore.
   b. copper.
   c. a gemstone.
   d. a native element.

_____ **16.** A favorable location for a wind farm is a
   a. river.
   b. mountain pass.
   c. rainforest.
   d. city.

_____ **17.** Fossil fuels consist primarily of
   a. anthracite.
   b. metals.
   c. gypsum.
   d. hydrocarbons.

_____ **18.** A substance that can be obtained through placer mining is
   a. coal.
   b. petroleum.
   c. gold.
   d. oil shale.

_____ **19.** The purpose of a catalytic converter is to
   a. reduce air pollution caused by auto emissions.
   b. use uranium to generate heat.
   c. make coal burn more cleanly.
   d. produce solar energy in photovoltaic cells.

_____ **20.** What happens during nuclear fusion?
   a. Fuel rods create nuclear energy.
   b. The nuclei of heavy atoms are split.
   c. Uranium-235 is processed into fuel pellets.
   d. The nuclei of hydrogen atoms combine.

Skills Worksheet

Concept Review

In the space provided, write the letter of the description that best matches the term or phrase.

_____ **1.** nonconformity

_____ **2.** unconformity

_____ **3.** varve

_____ **4.** law of crosscutting relationships

_____ **5.** radiometric dating

_____ **6.** disconformity

_____ **7.** trace fossil

_____ **8.** uniformitarianism

_____ **9.** law of superposition

_____ **10.** index fossil

a. sedimentary rock layers are younger than layers below

b. determining absolute age by comparing radioactive and stable isotopes

c. current geologic processes are the same as those that were at work in the past

d. stratified rock resting on unstratified rock

e. a fossilized mark formed by the movement of an animal

f. a fossil used to determine the age of rock layers

g. a break in the geologic record

h. a banded layer of sand and silt deposited annually in a lake

i. a fault or body of rock is younger than any other body of rock it cuts through

j. boundary between horizontal layers of sedimentary rock, and younger layers over an eroded surface

In the space provided, write the letter of the answer choice that best completes each statement or best answers each question.

_____ **11.** Using rates of erosion to determine absolute age is only practical for geologic features
  a. between 100,000 and 200,000 years old.
  b. between 10,000 and 20,000 years old.
  c. about 2 million years old.
  d. about 2 billion years old.

_____ **12.** Why is radioactive decay used to determine the actual age of rocks?
  a. Radioactive decay happens at a relatively constant rate.
  b. Radioactive decay happens slowly.
  c. Radioactive decay doesn't happen slowly.
  d. Radioactive decay doesn't happen at a relatively constant rate.

Name _____ Class _____ Date _____

Concept Review *continued*

_____ **13.** The age of an object in relation to the ages of other objects is its
     a. relative age.
     b. absolute age.
     c. cumulative age.
     d. comparable age.

_____ **14.** A break or crack in Earth's crust along which rocks shift their position is called a(n)
     a. intrusion.
     b. fault.
     c. crosscut.
     d. unconformity.

_____ **15.** In general, sedimentary rock is deposited at the rate of
     a. 30 cm over 1,000 years.
     b. 30 cm over 100 years.
     c. 30 m over 1,000 years.
     d. 30 m over 1 million years.

_____ **16.** A varve consists of a
     a. fine summer layer of sediment overlaid with a coarse winter layer.
     b. coarse summer layer of sediment over a fine winter layer.
     c. coarse summer layer of sediment overlaid with a fine winter layer.
     d. layer of coarse sediment deposited annually.

_____ **17.** Almost all fossils are discovered in
     a. igneous rock.
     b. metamorphic rock.
     c. sedimentary rock.
     d. organic materials.

_____ **18.** The study of fossils is called
     a. archeology.
     b. anthropology.
     c. geology.
     d. paleontology.

_____ **19.** Paleontologists examine coprolites to
     a. study replicas of the original organism.
     b. study the surface features of the original organism.
     c. help locate nearby dinosaur remains.
     d. learn about the feeding habits of dinosaurs.

_____ **20.** Geologists use index fossils to
     a. study organisms that existed in very small numbers.
     b. study organisms that lived during a long span of geologic time.
     c. study similar types of fossils.
     d. locate rock layers that contain oil and natural gas deposits.

Skills Worksheet

Concept Review

In the space provided, write the letter of the definition that best matches the term or phrase.

_____ 1. shield

_____ 2. nebula

_____ 3. evolution

_____ 4. geologic column

_____ 5. epoch

_____ 6. mass extinction

_____ 7. index fossil

_____ 8. period

_____ 9. geologic time scale

_____ 10. impact hypothesis

a. a fossil that is used to date rocks

b. a unit of geologic time that is longer than an age but shorter than a period

c. an episode during which an enormous number of species dies

d. a large area of exposed Precambrian rocks

e. a large cloud from which Earth formed

f. a theory that a meteorite caused the extinction of dinosaurs

g. the gradual development of new organisms from preexisting organisms

h. an ordered arrangement of rock layers

i. a unit of geologic time that is longer than an epoch but shorter than an era

j. a chart outlining the development Earth and life on Earth

In the space provided, write the letter of the answer choice that best completes each statement or best answers each question.

_____ 11. "206 Ma" means
   a. "in the year 206."
   b. "206 years ago."
   c. "206 thousand years ago."
   d. "206 million years ago."

_____ 12. Coastlines took on their present shapes during the
   a. Miocene Epoch.
   b. Pliocene Epoch.
   c. Holocene Epoch.
   d. Pleistocene Epoch.

_____ 13. The most common Cambrian invertebrates were called
   a. brachiopods.
   b. lungfish.
   c. jellyfish.
   d. trilobites.

_____ **14.** Which of the following animal species evolved during the
Paleocene Epoch?
   a. Homo sapiens
   b. fish
   c. primates
   d. cockroaches

_____ **15.** Dividing Precambrian time into smaller time units is difficult because
   a. it was a very short period.
   b. Precambrian fossils show a wide variety of life-forms.
   c. Earth went through few changes during this time.
   d. few fossils exist in early Precambrian rocks.

_____ **16.** Coal deposits in the eastern United States are the fossilized remains of
forests and swamps from the
   a. Permian Period.
   b. Carboniferous Period.
   c. Jurassic Period.
   d. Cretaceous Period.

_____ **17.** A mass extinction of marine invertebrates occurred at the end of the
Permian Period when
   a. a large meteorite landed on Earth.
   b. shallow inland seas disappeared.
   c. tectonic plates collided.
   d. volcanic activity increased.

_____ **18.** The climate during the Mesozoic Era was generally
   a. icy.
   b. hot and dry.
   c. cool and dry.
   d. warm and humid.

_____ **19.** The herbivore Apatosaurus belonged to the group of dinosaurs called
   a. saurischians.
   b. ornithischians.
   c. pterosaurs.
   d. ichthyosaurs.

_____ **20.** The division of geologic time that began with the last ice age and
includes the present is called the
   a. Cretaceous Period.
   b. Tertiary Period.
   c. Quaternary Period.
   d. Cenozoic Era.

Name _____ Class _____ Date _____

Concept Review

In the space provided, write the letter of the definition that best matches the term or phrase.

_____ **1.** Pangaea

_____ **2.** lithosphere

_____ **3.** rift valley

_____ **4.** sea-floor spreading

_____ **5.** paleomagnetism

_____ **6.** terrane

_____ **7.** mid-ocean ridge

_____ **8.** subduction zone

_____ **9.** continental drift

_____ **10.** convection cell

a. region along a plate boundary where one plate moves under another

b. piece of lithosphere with a unique geologic history

c. crack in the center of a mid-ocean ridge

d. supercontinent formed about 300 million years ago

e. residual magnetism of rock

f. process by which new sea floor forms

g. layer that forms the thin outer shell of Earth

h. cycle in which heated material rises and cooler material sinks

i. undersea mountain range

j. hypothesis that the continents once formed a single landmass

In the space provided, write the letter of the answer choice that best completes each statement or best answers each question.

_____ **11.** What kind of fossil evidence supported Wegener's hypothesis?
   a. fossils hinting at a land bridge between South America and Africa
   b. fossils proving Mesosaurus never lived in Africa
   c. plant fossils showing that cold areas used to be tropical
   d. sea fossils proving the continents had plowed through the ocean floor

_____ **12.** Sea-floor spreading was a key discovery because it showed
   a. that mid-ocean ridges exist.
   b. how continents move.
   c. why some rocks have reversed polarity.
   d. that mid-ocean ridges have rifts at the center.

_____ **13.** Tectonic plates ride on the layer of Earth's mantle called the
   a. lithosphere.
   b. oceanic crust.
   c. continental crust.
   d. asthenosphere.

Concept Review *continued*

_____ **14.** Scientists identify tectonic plate boundaries primarily by studying
   a. the outlines of the continents.
   b. earthquake data.
   c. the Pacific Ring of Fire.
   d. active volcanoes.

_____ **15.** A plate boundary at which two plates slide past each other horizontally is a
   a. divergent boundary.
   b. convergent boundary.
   c. transform boundary.
   d. subduction zone.

_____ **16.** Convection currents cause movement of tectonic plates by
   a. making water in Earth's core boil.
   b. creating ridge push and slab pull.
   c. making hot mantle material sink.
   d. turning lithosphere to asthenosphere.

_____ **17.** New, smaller continents may form from larger continents through
   a. rifting.
   b. accretion.
   c. paleomagnetism.
   d. subduction.

_____ **18.** What often forms when large terranes and continents collide?
   a. mid-ocean ridges
   b. atolls
   c. seamounts
   d. major mountain chains

_____ **19.** The movements of the continents
   a. discourage the development of unique species.
   b. keep climates constant.
   c. create fewer mountain ranges.
   d. isolate some populations of organisms.

_____ **20.** One likely result of the supercontinent cycle is that
   a. the continents will continue to get further apart.
   b. California will move closer to the equator.
   c. the Mediterranean Sea will close.
   d. the Atlantic Ocean will disappear.

Name _____ Class _____ Date _____

Concept Review

In the space provided, write the letter of the description that best matches the term or phrase.

_____ 1. shear stress

_____ 2. folded mountain

_____ 3. isostasy

_____ 4. fault-block mountain

_____ 5. dome mountain

_____ 6. fault

_____ 7. compression

_____ 8. tension

_____ 9. fold

_____ 10. mountain range

a. stress that stretches and pulls a body of rock apart

b. a series of mountains related in shape and structure

c. a bend in rock layers from stress

d. distorts by pushing parts of the body in opposite directions

e. mountain formed when rock layers are squeezed and uplifted

f. equilibrium in gravity and buoyancy between the asthenosphere and the lithosphere

g. a break in rock where surrounding rock slides

h. stress that squeezes and shortens rock

i. forms where faults break Earth's crust into large blocks that tilt and drop

j. mountain with rock layers sloping from a central point

In the space provided, write the letter of the answer choice that best completes each statement or best answers each question.

_____ 11. What are four types of mountains?
   a. fretted, faulted, superdome, volcano
   b. shear, vertical, horizontal, plateau
   c. grabens, plateau, valley, peak
   d. folded, fault-block, dome, volcanic

_____ 12. How do folded mountains form?
   a. tectonic movements squeeze rock layers
   b. tectonic movements make large blocks
   c. tectonic plates pull apart
   d. tectonic plates stretch and pull rock layers

_____ **13.** What happens when continental and oceanic lithospheres collide?
  a. Deep ocean trenches are formed.
  b. The oceanic lithosphere subducts beneath the continental lithosphere.
  c. Large blocks of rock are broken loose.
  d. The continental lithosphere subducts beneath the oceanic lithosphere.

_____ **14.** What happens when two oceanic plates collide?
  a. The plates come to a standstill.
  b. The lighter plate subducts beneath the other plate.
  c. The denser plate subducts beneath the other plate.
  d. They both subduct, forming a deep trench.

_____ **15.** When two continents collide,
  a. an oceanic deformation will result.
  b. both continents will be subducted.
  c. one continent will be subducted.
  d. the resulting uplift can form mountains.

_____ **16.** Where do volcanic mountains commonly form?
  a. along convergent plate boundaries
  b. away from plate boundaries
  c. along divergent plate boundaries
  d. at high elevations

_____ **17.** What is deformation?
  a. folding of the asthenosphere
  b. bending, tilting, and breaking of Earth's crust
  c. collision and divergence
  d. equilibrium in the crust

_____ **18.** What is strain?
  a. stretching of rock
  b. any change in rock from stress
  c. the same as stress
  d. rock being pulled apart

_____ **19.** Plateaus are
  a. folded mountains.
  b. large, flat areas of rock below sea level.
  c. large, flat areas of rock high above sea level.
  d. flat mountains.

_____ **20.** The sloping sides of a fold are called
  a. layers.
  b. legs.
  c. hinges.
  d. limbs.

Skills Worksheet

Concept Review

In the space provided, write the letter of the description that best matches the term or phrase.

_____ 1. seismic gap

_____ 2. Richter scale

_____ 3. body wave

_____ 4. tsunami

_____ 5. modified Mercalli scale

_____ 6. surface wave

_____ 7. seismograph

_____ 8. foreshock

_____ 9. elastic rebound

_____ 10. moment magnitude

a. an instrument used for detecting and recording vibrations in the ground

b. a measurement of earthquake strength based on the size of the area of the fault that moves

c. a scale expressing earthquake intensity

d. a wave that travels through the body of a medium

e. a scale that measures the ground motion from earthquakes

f. the sudden return of deformed rock to its undeformed state

g. a wave that travels along the surface of a body, not through the middle

h. a fault area where few quakes have occurred recently, but where strong quakes have occurred in the past

i. a little earthquake that precedes a larger one

j. a giant wave that can form after an undersea earthquake

In the space provided, write the letter of the answer choice that best completes each statement or best answers each question.

_____ 11. What can happen to tall buildings during an earthquake?
a. They can crack and implode.
b. The windows can blow out from the inside.
c. Nothing usually happens.
d. They can sway and even tip over.

_____ 12. If you are inside during an earthquake,
a. lie down in an open area.
b. call 911.
c. get outside as quickly as possible.
d. stand in a doorway or crouch under a desk.

_____ **13.** Why do seismic waves speed up at about 30 km beneath the surface of continents?
   a. because Earth's mantle is denser than the crust
   b. because of Earth's magnetic field
   c. because Earth's crust is denser than the mantle
   d. because of the force of gravity

_____ **14.** Why do earthquakes usually occur at plate boundaries?
   a. because stress on the rocks is least at the boundaries
   b. because of gravity pushing down on the plates
   c. because the stress on the rocks of the plates is greatest at the boundaries
   d. because of the magnetic qualities of the plates

_____ **15.** If you are in a car during an earthquake, you should
   a. stop away from structures that might collapse.
   b. get inside a building.
   c. get out of the car.
   d. drive away quickly.

_____ **16.** When an earthquake occurs,
   a. run as fast as you can.   **c.** get inside a building.
   b. stay calm.   **d.** panic.

_____ **17.** How do scientists find the distance to an epicenter?
   a. by analyzing departure times of P waves and S waves
   b. by graphing P waves and Q waves
   c. by measuring distances in kilometers
   d. by analyzing arrival times of P waves and S waves

_____ **18.** Scientists monitor natural gas seepage from rocks because
   a. it may cause earthquakes.
   b. it may mean trouble.
   c. it may indicate seismic activity.
   d. it may indicate the presence of oil.

_____ **19.** Where does the first motion of an earthquake occur?
   a. at the focus
   b. at the center
   c. in the fault zone
   d. in the crust

_____ **20.** What is another name for a P wave?
   a. a proper wave
   b. a secondary wave
   c. a tidal wave
   d. a primary wave

Skills Worksheet

Concept Review

In the space provided, write the letter of the definition that best matches the term or phrase.

_____ **1.** magma

_____ **2.** volcanism

_____ **3.** lava

_____ **4.** volcano

_____ **5.** hot spot

_____ **6.** mafic

_____ **7.** felsic

_____ **8.** pyroclastic material

_____ **9.** caldera

_____ **10.** cinder cone

a. magma that flows onto Earth's surface; the rock that forms when lava cools and solidifies

b. describes magma or igneous rock that is rich in feldspar and silica and that is generally light in color

c. liquid rock produced under Earth's surface

d. describes magma or igneous rock that is rich in magnesium and iron and that is generally dark in color

e. a vent or fissure in Earth's surface through which magma and gases are expelled

f. a volcanically active area of Earth's surface, commonly far from a tectonic plate boundary

g. any activity that includes the movement of magma toward or onto Earth's surface

h. a large, circular depression that forms when the magma chamber below a volcano partially empties and causes the ground above to sink

i. a type of volcano that has very steep slopes

j. fragments of rock that form during a volcanic eruption

In the space provided, write the letter of the answer choice that best completes each statement or best answers each question.

_____ **11.** Magma can change form when
   a. the outside temperature changes.
   b. the tectonic plates shift.
   c. water is added to hot rock.
   d. an earthquake occurs.

_____ **12.** Volcanism is common at convergent and divergent boundaries of
   a. tectonic plates.
   b. continents.
   c. oceans.
   d. vents.

_____ **13.** Hot spots are areas of volcanic activity located over rising
   a. gases.
   b. lava.
   c. calderas.
   d. mantle plumes.

| Concept Review *continued*

_____ **14.** This type of mafic lava flow forms a wrinkly, rope-like texture when it cools.
   a. blocky lava
   b. aa
   c. pluton
   d. pahoehoe

_____ **15.** Volcanoes take place in zones near convergent and divergent boundaries of tectonic plates, in subduction zones, and in
   a. cinder cones.
   b. mountainous areas.
   c. mid-ocean ridges.
   d. flood zones.

_____ **16.** When magma cools and solidifies inside the crust, it causes large formations of igneous rock called
   a. plutons.
   b. plumes.
   c. intrusives.
   d. fractures.

_____ **17.** Thick, sticky magma, high in viscosity and trapped gases, causes
   a. quiet eruptions.
   b. explosive eruptions.
   c. no eruptions.
   d. most eruptions.

_____ **18.** The largest type of pyroclastic material is
   a. volcanic dust.
   b. volcanic blocks.
   c. lapilli.
   d. volcanic bombs.

_____ **19.** Which of the following is NOT a type of volcano?
   a. shield
   b. composite
   c. crater
   d. cinder cone

_____ **20.** Which of the following does NOT signal a volcanic eruption?
   a. change in earthquake activity
   b. change in volcano shape
   c. change in composition and amount of gases emitted
   d. changes in ocean temperature

Name _____ Class _____ Date _____

Skills Worksheet

Concept Review

In the space provided, write the letter of the definition that best matches the term or phrase.

_____ 1. horizon

_____ 2. erosion

_____ 3. oxidation

_____ 4. abrasion

_____ 5. mechanical weathering

_____ 6. soil profile

_____ 7. chemical weathering

_____ 8. differential weathering

_____ 9. topography

_____ 10. solifluction

a. the process by which rocks break down as a result of chemical reactions

b. a process in which the materials of Earth's surface are loosened, dissolved, or worn away and transported from one place to another by a natural agent, such as wind, water, ice, or gravity

c. a vertical section of soil that shows the layers of horizons

d. a reaction that removes one or more electrons from a substance such that the substance's valence or oxidation state increases

e. the process by which softer, less weather resistant rocks wear away at a faster rather than harder, more weather resistant rocks do

f. the elevation or slope of land; affects the rate of weathering

g. the process by which rocks break down into smaller pieces by physical means

h. the grinding and wearing away of rock surfaces through the mechanical action of other rock or sand particles

i. the slow, downslope flow of soil saturated with water in areas surrounding glaciers at high elevations

j. a horizontal layer of soil that can be distinguished from the layers above and below it; also a boundary between two rock layers that have different physical properties

In the space provided, write the letter of the answer choice that best completes each statement or best answers each question.

_____ 11. Which landforms are NOT typical in hot, dry climates?
   a. buttes
   b. round hills
   c. mesas
   d. plateaus

_____ 12. Which of the following does NOT involve a chemical process that decomposes rock?
   a. carbonation
   b. hydrolysis
   c. ice wedging
   d. acid precipitation

Name _____ Class _____ Date _____

Concept Review *continued*

_____ **13.** The layer of rock fragments that covers much of Earth's surface is called
    a. bedrock.
    b. regolith.
    c. humus.
    d. pedalfer.

_____ **14.** Climates that have the fastest rates of weathering
    a. are hot and dry.
    b. are warm and humid.
    c. alternate between hot and cold.
    d. are cold and dry.

_____ **15.** Which of the following is NOT a farming method that conserves soil?
    a. terracing
    b. strip-cropping
    c. crop dusting
    d. contour plowing

_____ **16.** The rock from which soil was weathered, and upon which the characteristics of soil mainly depend on, is called
    a. igneous.
    b. bedrock.
    c. limestone.
    d. parent rock.

_____ **17.** When a rock's exposure to weathering agents increases,
    a. the rock weathers faster.
    b. the rock weathers more slowly.
    c. the rock stops weathering.
    d. the rock produces nitric acid.

_____ **18.** The various layers of soil—topsoil, subsoil, and bedrock—can be viewed and studied in
    a. humus.
    b. transported soil.
    c. residual soil
    d. a soil profile.

_____ **19.** Soil characteristic of desert and arctic regions is
    a. thick and fertile.
    b. thin and fertile.
    c. thick and nutrient-poor.
    d. thin and nutrient-poor.

_____ **20.** In which of these events is gravity a factor in erosion?
    a. abrasion   **c.** dust storm
    b. sheet erosion   **d.** slump

Skills Worksheet

Concept Review

In the space provided, write the letter of the description that best matches the term or phrase.

_____ **1.** condensation

_____ **2.** floodplain

_____ **3.** watershed

_____ **4.** tributary

_____ **5.** evapotranspiration

_____ **6.** discharge

_____ **7.** desalination

_____ **8.** delta

_____ **9.** precipitation

_____ **10.** alluvial fan

a. any form of water that falls to Earth's surface from the clouds, including rain, snow, sleet, and hail

b. change of state from a gas to a liquid

c. the process of removing salt from ocean water

d. area along a river, formed by sediments deposited when the river overflows its banks

e. fan-shaped mass of rock material deposited by a stream on land where the slope decreases sharply

f. area of land drained by a river system

g. fan-shaped mass of rock material deposited at the mouth of a stream into another body of water

h. volume of water moved by a stream in a given time period

i. the total water loss from an area by evaporation and transpiration

j. stream that flows into a lake or into a larger stream

In the space provided, write the letter of the answer choice that best completes each statement or best answers each question.

_____ **11.** A river system begins to form in a given area when
   a. evapotranspiration exceeds precipitation.
   b. precipitation exceeds evapotranspiration.
   c. precipitation exceeds condensation.
   d. condensation exceeds precipitation.

_____ **12.** What happens over time as a stream's channel erodes?
   a. The stream becomes a watershed.
   b. The stream becomes a valley.
   c. The stream becomes a river
   d. The stream dries out.

Name _____ Class _____ Date _____

Concept Review *continued*

_____ **13.** When precipitation exceeds evapotranspiration and runoff,
  a. soil becomes dry and irrigation is necessary.
  b. soil becomes moist and wind increases.
  c. soil becomes dry and flooding is possible.
  d. soil becomes moist and flooding is possible.

_____ **14.** Which of the following factors affect the water budget?
  a. temperature, vegetation, wind, rainfall
  b. rock formation, conservation, rainfall, supply costs
  c. purification costs, water management, conservation, rainfall
  d. desalination, conservation, cost of land, rainfall

_____ **15.** Which of the following are stages of the water cycle?
  a. transportation, deposition, precipitation
  b. evapotranspiration, condensation, precipitation
  c. evaporation, transmutation, participation
  d. transubstantiation, condensation, precession

_____ **16.** Why do people choose to live in floodplains?
  a. There is access to fishing and the soil is rich.
  b. Floods can be overcome.
  c. Water drainage is good.
  d. The soil is good for housing development.

_____ **17.** Which of the following are methods of water conservation?
  a. encouraging pollution
  b. damming rivers
  c. reducing evaporation and condensation
  d. enforcing conservation laws

_____ **18.** Which of the following affect erosion caused by a river?
  a. acid rain and pollution
  b. rocks and sand
  c. discharge and gradient
  d. watersheds and floods

_____ **19.** Which is a direct method of flood control?
  a. soil conservation
  b. dam
  c. natural levee
  d. valley

_____ **20.** A lake forms when
  a. two or more rivers meet.
  b. a river runs dry.
  c. condensation occurs.
  d. precipitation collects in a depression.

Skills Worksheet

Concept Review

In the space provided, write the letter of the definition that best matches the term or phrase.

_____ **1.** artesian formation

_____ **2.** groundwater

_____ **3.** permeability

_____ **4.** porosity

_____ **5.** aquifer

_____ **6.** water table

_____ **7.** karst topography

_____ **8.** cavern

_____ **9.** sinkhole

_____ **10.** hard water

a. water with high concentrations of dissolved minerals

b. a large cave consisting of many smaller connecting chambers

c. a circular depression that forms at the surface when rock dissolves, sediment is removed, or caves collapse

d. a system of caverns, sinkholes, and underground drainage

e. water beneath Earth's surface

f. a body of rock that stores and allows the flow of underground water

g. the percentage of the total volume of rock consisting of open spaces

h. the ability of rock to let water flow through its open spaces

i. the upper surface of underground water

j. the sloping layer of permeable rock between two layers of impermeable rock that is exposed at the surface

In the space provided, write the letter of the answer choice that best completes each statement or best answers each question.

_____ **11.** Rock or sediment with low porosity is characterized by
  a. poorly sorted particles of different sizes.
  b. well-sorted, fine-grained particles.
  c. well-sorted, coarse-grained particles.
  d. loosely packed particles.

_____ **12.** Groundwater flows downward in response to
  a. porosity.
  b. gravity.
  c. topography.
  d. capillary pull.

_____ **13.** The zone of aeration is composed of how many regions?
  a. one
  b. two
  c. three
  d. four

_____ **14.** Weak acid formed by the passage of water through soil causes
    a. capillary action.
    b. aeration.
    c. chemical weathering.
    d. saturation.

_____ **15.** Two land features formed by hot groundwater are hot springs and
    a. sinkholes.
    b. stalactites.
    c. stalagmites.
    d. geysers.

_____ **16.** Two of the most important properties of aquifers that affect the flow of groundwater are porosity and
    a. permeability.
    b. sorting.
    c. sediment.
    d. packing.

_____ **17.** How does the water table relate to surface topography?
    a. The water table usually mirrors surface topography.
    b. The water table is not affected by surface topography.
    c. The water table is similar to surface topography in dry regions.
    d. The water table takes shape according to the porosity of the rock.

_____ **18.** A hole dug below the water level in order to bring water to the surface is called a(n)
    a. spring.
    b. artesian feature.
    c. depression.
    d. well.

_____ **19.** What is a natural flow of water to the surface where the surface dips below the water table?
    a. cone
    b. spring
    c. geyser
    d. well

_____ **20.** A sloping layer of permeable rock captured between two layers of impermeable rock is called a(n)
    a. artesian formation.
    b. caprock.
    c. spring.
    d. geyser.

Skills Worksheet

Concept Review

In the space provided, write the letter of the description that best matches the term or phrase.

_____ 1. snowfield

_____ 2. ice shelf

_____ 3. cirque

_____ 4. esker

_____ 5. glacier

_____ 6. internal plastic flow

_____ 7. erratic

_____ 8. interglacial period

_____ 9. precession

_____ 10. alpine glacier

a. a narrow glacier formed in a mountainous region

b. part of an ice sheet that moves over the ocean

c. a wobble in Earth's axis

d. a large rock transported by a glacier from a distant source

e. the process by which glaciers flow as ice grains deform under pressure and slide over each other

f. a bowl-shaped depression formed by glacial erosion

g. a long, winding ridge of stratified drift

h. a large mass of moving ice

i. an almost motionless mass of permanent snow and ice

j. a period of warmer climate during which glaciers retreat

In the space provided, write the letter of the answer choice that best completes each statement or best answers each question.

_____ 11. Which of the following features form when tension and compression build under the surface of a flowing glacier?
  a. crevasses
  b. ice shelves
  c. kettles
  d. roches moutonnées

_____ 12. Ice in a glacier moves downslope in response to
  a. friction.
  b. melting.
  c. gravity.
  d. freezing.

_____ 13. Which of the following features is caused by erosion rather than by deposition?
  a. drumlin
  b. kettle
  c. esker
  d. horn

_____ 14. A moraine is an example of a(n)
  a. sorted glacial deposit.
  b. unsorted glacial deposit.
  c. erosional feature caused by moving ice.
  d. erosional feature caused by moving water.

_____ **15.** Which of the following are needed to form a salt lake?
    a. periods of low temperatures
    b. high precipitation rates
    c. multiple outlet streams
    d. rapid evaporation rates

_____ **16.** Where has evidence of past ice ages been found?
    a. in outwash plains
    b. in glacial crevasses
    c. on mountaintops
    d. in shells of dead marine animals

_____ **17.** What is till?
    a. sorted deposits of rock material
    b. unsorted glacial drift
    c. sorted deposits of sand
    d. sediment sorted by melted ice

_____ **18.** Which of the following probably occurs before an ice age begins?
    a. longer interglacial periods
    b. a rise in sea level
    c. a slow drop in global temperatures
    d. a decrease in precipitation

_____ **19.** Which of the following does the Milankovitch theory consider to be factors in the cause of ice ages?
    a. changes in the amount of radiation produced by the sun
    b. blockage of the sun's rays by volcanic dust
    c. movement of continents, which affects warm ocean currents
    d. small changes in Earth's orbit, tilt, and precession

_____ **20.** Which of the following occurs when a glacier moves by basal slip?
    a. A glacier's weight melts ice where it touches the ground.
    b. Meltwater flows beneath a glacier.
    c. Deformed grains of ice slide over each other.
    d. Warmer temperatures at the glacier's surface melt ice.

Concept Review

In the space provided, write the letter of the description that best matches each term or phrase.

_____ 1. lagoon

_____ 2. deflation

_____ 3. beach

_____ 4. estuary

_____ 5. loess

_____ 6. headland

_____ 7. ventifact

_____ 8. fiord

_____ 9. transverse dune

_____ 10. saltation

a. fine-grained sediment formed by the accumulation of windblown dust

b. deep bay with steep walls

c. sand ridge that forms at a right angle to wind direction

d. region of shallow water between a barrier island and the shoreline

e. form of erosion in which fine, dry soil particles are blown away

f. resistant rock formation that projects out from shore

g. process by which wind moves sand along the ground

h. area of shoreline made up of deposited sediment

i. bay in which salt water and fresh water mix

j. rock smoothed by wind erosion

In the space provided, write the letter of the answer choice that best completes each statement or best answers each question.

_____ 11. The feature formed when sea level rises or land sinks is called a(n)
   a. emergent coastline.
   b. fiord.
   c. submergent coastline.
   d. lagoon.

_____ 12. Rock particles that remain after deflation occurs often form
   a. deflation hollows.
   b. ventifacts.
   c. barchan dunes.
   d. desert pavement, or stone pavement.

_____ 13. Which of the following is the result of wave erosion?
   a. sea cliff
   b. berm
   c. barchan dune
   d. beach

_____ 14. During dune migration, sand moves over the dune crest and builds up on the
   a. fiord.
   b. headland.
   c. slipface.
   d. berm.

_____ **15.** The abrasive action of waves that reduces rocks to small pebbles and sand grains is called
  a. chemical weathering.
  b. deflation.
  c. saltation.
  d. mechanical weathering.

_____ **16.** When an emergent coastline forms and it has a gentle slope, the coastline will feature
  a. long, wide beaches.
  b. bays or headlands.
  c. sea cliffs.
  d. narrow inlets.

_____ **17.** Which of the following causes a change in absolute sea level?
  a. movement of Earth's crust
  b. movement of tectonic plates
  c. change in the amount of ocean water
  d. change in pollution level

_____ **18.** A longshore current produces sand deposits called
  a. beaches and berms.
  b. spits and tombolos.
  c. sea caves and arches.
  d. estuaries and fiords.

_____ **19.** Coastal lands can be preserved by
  a. eroding barrier islands.
  b. slowing development.
  c. draining lagoons.
  d. increasing pollution risk.

_____ **20.** A sea cave forms when
  a. waves erode the base of a sea cliff.
  b. sand moves along the shore.
  c. Earth's crust moves.
  d. a wave-cut terrace collapses.

Name _____ Class _____ Date _____

Concept Review

In the space provided, write the letter of the definition that best matches the term or phrase.

_____ **1.** abyssal plain

_____ **2.** continental shelf

_____ **3.** mid-ocean ridge

_____ **4.** continental slope

_____ **5.** guyot

_____ **6.** continental rise

_____ **7.** submarine canyon

_____ **8.** seamount

_____ **9.** trench

_____ **10.** fracture zone

a. flat-topped, submerged seamount

b. underwater mountain range

c. rough topography across an underwater ridge

d. the part of the continent covered by water

e. flat area of deep-ocean basin

f. deep, v-shaped underwater valley

g. steep slope from the continental shelf to the ocean

h. submerged volcanic mountain taller than 1 km

i. raised wedge at the base of a continental slope

j. long, narrow depression in deep-ocean basin

In the space provided, write the letter of the answer choice that best completes each statement or best answers each question.

_____ **11.** Some inorganic sediments in the ocean basin come from
   a. radiolarians.
   b. nodules.
   c. icebergs.
   d. foraminiferans.

_____ **12.** The deepest of Earth's major oceans is the
   a. Atlantic.
   b. Pacific.
   c. Indian.
   d. Southern.

_____ **13.** Sediments are spread over wide areas of the deep-ocean basins by
   a. nodules.
   b. core samples.
   c. turbidity currents.
   d. wave erosion.

_____ **14.** Deep-ocean floor sediment that is formed from the shells of
radiolarians and diatoms is
  a. mud.
  b. calcareous ooze.
  c. siliceous ooze.
  d. foraminiferans.

_____ **15.** Oceanographers can use sonar to calculate the depth of the ocean
floor because
  a. sound waves can penetrate the ocean floor.
  b. echoes do not travel through sea water.
  c. sound waves travel about 1,500 m/s through sea water.
  d. sound waves bounce off the ocean floor.

_____ **16.** A research vessel that goes deep in the ocean but remains connected
to the research ship is a
  a. submarine robot.
  b. drilling ship.
  c. bathyscaph.
  d. bathysphere.

_____ **17.** An example of a sea is the
  a. Indian.
  b. Caribbean.
  c. Arctic.
  d. Southern.

_____ **18.** Which is caused by glacial periods?
  a. The continental shelf erodes.
  b. Submarine canyons form in the continental shelf.
  c. Water covers the continental shelf.
  d. The continental shelf grows smaller.

_____ **19.** Which is NOT a source of deep-ocean basin sediment?
  a. icebergs
  b. volcanoes
  c. meteorites
  d. earthquakes

_____ **20.** A deep-ocean floor sediment that consists of at least 40% clay particles
is a form of
  a. calcareous ooze.
  b. red clay mud.
  c. nodule.
  d. siliceous ooze.

Skills Worksheet

Concept Review

In the space provided, write the letter of the description that best matches the term or phrase.

_____ 1. nitrogen, oxygen, and carbon dioxide

_____ 2. salinity

_____ 3. pack ice

_____ 4. ocean temperature

_____ 5. thermocline

_____ 6. density

_____ 7. ocean color

_____ 8. plankton

_____ 9. food, minerals, fresh water

_____ 10. mercury, insecticide, and DDT

a. the ratio of the mass of a substance to the volume of the substance; commonly expressed as grams per cubic centimeter for solids and as grams per liter for gases

b. the foundation of life in the ocean

c. this measurement is affected by the amount of solar energy an area receives and by the movement of water

d. by studying variations in this, scientists can determine the presence of phytoplankton in the ocean

e. atmospheric gases that are also the main gases found in ocean water

f. a layer in a body of water in which water temperature drops with increased depth faster than it does in other areas

g. important resources of the ocean

h. major pollutants in the ocean

i. a measure of the amount of dissolved salts in a given amount of liquid

j. a floating layer of sea ice that completely covers an area of the ocean surface

In the space provided, write the letter of the answer choice that best completes each statement or best answers each question.

_____ 11. Marine organisms help maintain the chemical balance of ocean water by removing nutrients and gases from the ocean and
a. returning other nutrients and gases to the water.
b. producing bacteria that destroy pollutants.
c. adding no new elements to the water.
d. introducing minerals and trace elements to the water.

_____ 12. Plankton can be called "the foundation of life in the ocean" because they
a. are marine organisms that need sunlight.
b. live in the upper 100 m of water.
c. form the base of complex food webs in the ocean.
d. are one of three main food sources in the ocean.

Concept Review *continued*

_____ **13.** This type of ocean water dissolves gases most easily.
     a. cold
     b. warm
     c. shallow
     d. salty

_____ **14.** Why is the ocean called a carbon sink?
     a. Ocean water destroys trace carbon elements.
     b. Organisms in the water release carbon dioxide into the air.
     c. Ocean water dissolves carbon dioxide from the atmosphere.
     d. Ocean water becomes more salty with high carbon levels.

_____ **15.** In the benthic zone of the ocean, you might find
     a. dolphins.
     b. whales.
     c. swordfish.
     d. starfish.

_____ **16.** In the pelagic zone of the ocean, you might find
     a. sponges.
     b. tuna.
     c. worms.
     d. octopuses.

_____ **17.** Which of the following items is NOT a means of obtaining fresh water from the ocean?
     a. aquaculture
     b. desalination
     c. freezing
     d. reverse osmosis desalination

_____ **18.** Which of the following sea life is an example of nekton?
     a. oysters
     b. cod
     c. plankton
     d. sea stars

_____ **19.** Which of the following sea life is an example of benthos?
     a. plankton
     b. dolphins
     c. squid
     d. crabs

_____ **20.** The most valuable resource found in the ocean is
     a. salt.
     b. petroleum.
     c. fish.
     d. trace elements.

Skills Worksheet

Concept Review

In the space provided, write the letter of the definition that best matches the term or phrase.

_____ **1.** gyre

_____ **2.** tidal current

_____ **3.** Gulf Stream

_____ **4.** deep current

_____ **5.** wave

_____ **6.** refraction

_____ **7.** tidal oscillation

_____ **8.** Coriolis effect

_____ **9.** wave period

_____ **10.** surface current

a. swift, warm Atlantic current that flows along the eastern United States

b. movement of water toward and away from the coast caused by rising and falling tides

c. streamlike movement of ocean water far below the surface

d. time required for two consecutive wave crests to pass a given point

e. huge circle of moving ocean water found above and below the equator

f. curving of the path of oceans and winds due to Earth's rotation

g. horizontal movement of ocean water at or near the ocean's surface that is caused by winds

h. process by which ocean waves bend toward the coastline as they approach shallow water

i. slow, rocking motion of ocean water that occurs as tidal bulges move around the ocean basins

j. periodic disturbance in a solid, liquid, or gas as energy is transmitted through a medium

In the space provided, write the letter of the answer choice that best completes each statement or best answers each question.

_____ **11.** A force that pushes currents westward across the tropical latitudes of all three major oceans is called
    a. gravity.
    b. Gulf Stream.
    c. trade winds.
    d. westerlies.

_____ **12.** The deep current that moves slowly northward along the ocean bottom to a latitude of about 40°N is the
    a. Sargasso Sea.
    b. Antarctic Circumpolar Current.
    c. Antarctic Bottom Water.
    d. North Atlantic Current.

_____ **13.** A breaker forms when
   a. the bottom of a wave is slowed by friction and the top of the wave continues moving at its original speed.
   b. energy is transferred from the air to the ocean.
   c. the path of oceans and winds curves.
   d. cooling water contracts.

_____ **14.** Most tsunamis are caused by
   a. wind.
   b. earthquakes on the ocean floor.
   c. the gravitational force of the moon.
   d. turbidity currents.

_____ **15.** How do you calculate the speed of a wave?
   a. Divide the wave period by its wavelength.
   b. Divide the wavelength by the wave period.
   c. Multiply the wave height by the wavelength.
   d. Divide the wavelength by the wave height.

_____ **16.** The movement of the tidal current when it flows toward the ocean is called
   a. slack water.
   b. flood tide.
   c. ebb tide.
   d. tidal bore.

_____ **17.** The gravitational pull of the moon on Earth and Earth's waters causes
   a. gyres.
   b. monsoons.
   c. the Coriolis effect.
   d. tides.

_____ **18.** What happens to the diameter of a water molecule's circular motion in a wave?
   a. It increases as water depth decreases.
   b. It decreases as water depth increases.
   c. It increases, decreases, and then increases again as depth decreases.
   d. It does not change as water depth changes.

_____ **19.** Which of the following tides occur during both the new moon and the full moon?
   a. spring tides
   b. neap tides
   c. tidal waves
   d. flood tides

_____ **20.** Which of the following describes the type of tides that occur each day along the U.S. Atlantic Coast?
   a. one high tide and one low tide
   b. one very high tide followed by two lower high tides
   c. two high tides and two low tides
   d. one high tide and two low tides

Skills Worksheet

Concept Review

In the space provided, write the letter of the description that best matches the term or phrase.

_____ **1.** layers of the atmosphere

_____ **2.** radiation

_____ **3.** conduction

_____ **4.** convection

_____ **5.** Coriolis effect

_____ **6.** global winds

_____ **7.** trade winds

_____ **8.** westerlies

_____ **9.** polar easterlies

_____ **10.** front

a. all forms of energy that travel through space as waves

b. prevailing winds that blow from west to east between 30° and 60° latitude in both hemispheres

c. the curving of the path of a moving object from an otherwise straight path due to Earth's rotation

d. troposophere; stratosphere; mesosphere; thermosphere

e. polar easterlies meet warm air from the westerlies, creating a stormy area

f. the transfer of energy as heat through a material

g. prevailing winds that blow from east to west between 60° and 90° latitude in both hemispheres

h. prevailing winds that blow from 30° to 0° latitude in both hemispheres

i. looping patterns of air flow, called convection cells, that move from the poles to the equator

j. the movement of matter due to differences in density that are caused by temperature variations; can result in the transfer of energy as heat

In the space provided, write the letter of the answer choice that best completes each statement or best answers each question.

_____ **11.** The atmosphere is a mixture of gases that surround Earth. Which of the following is NOT a gaseous component of the atmosphere?
  a. carbon dioxide   **c.** particulates
  b. argon   **d.** nitrogen

_____ **12.** Atmospheric pressure presses on the liquid mercury in a well of this instrument. The mercury rises in a tube as the atmospheric pressure rises. What is this instrument?
  a. mercurial barometer   **c.** aneroid barometer
  b. altimeter   **d.** thermometer

| Concept Review *continued*

_____ **13.** Changes in atmospheric pressure cause the sides of this instrument to bend inward or outward. Changes are measured on a scale. What is this instrument?
   a. mercurial barometer
   b. altimeter
   c. aneroid barometer
   d. thermometer

_____ **14.** All radiant energy reaches earth as a form of
   a. light waves.
   b. sound waves.
   c. electromagnetic waves.
   d. ultraviolet waves.

_____ **15.** Solar energy warms Earth when radiation is
   a. reflected.
   b. refracted.
   c. scattered.
   d. absorbed.

_____ **16.** Which of the following affects local wind patterns?
   a. trade winds
   b. local temperature variations
   c. solar storms
   d. season changes

_____ **17.** The gas that makes up most of Earth's atmosphere is
   a. oxygen.
   b. argon.
   c. nitrogen.
   d. ozone.

_____ **18.** All of the following are particulates EXCEPT
   a. carbon dioxide.
   b. salt particles.
   c. volcanic ash.
   d. pollen.

_____ **19.** The atmospheric layer that is closest to Earth and is where all weather conditions exist is the
   a. troposphere.   **c.** stratosphere.
   b. mesosphere.   **d.** thermosphere.

_____ **20.** The main source of air pollution is
   a. the nitrogen cycle.
   b. temperature inversions.
   c. smog.
   d. the burning of fossil fuels.

Name _____ Class _____ Date _____

Concept Review

In the space provided, write the letter of the definition that best matches the term or phrase.

_____ 1. sublimation

_____ 2. precipitation

_____ 3. cloud

_____ 4. dew point

_____ 5. fog

_____ 6. condensation nucleus

_____ 7. latent heat

_____ 8. absolute humidity

_____ 9. relative humidity

_____ 10. coalescence

a. a suspended particle that provides a surface for condensation

b. formation of a large droplet by the combination of small droplets

c. the temperature at which condensation equals evaporation

d. collection of water droplets or ice crystals suspended in the air

e. heat energy that is absorbed or released during a phase change

f. the mass of water vapor contained in a given volume of air

g. the process by which a solid changes directly into a gas

h. a mass of water vapor that condenses near the surface of Earth

i. any form of water that falls to Earth's surface from clouds

j. the ratio of actual water vapor content of the air to the amount of water vapor needed to reach saturation

In the space provided, write the letter of the answer choice that best completes each statement or best answers each question.

_____ 11. What is a low-altitude billowy cloud called?
   a. a stratus cloud
   b. a cumulus cloud
   c. a cirrus cloud
   d. fog

_____ 12. Water vapor changes into a liquid in the process of
   a. evaporation.
   b. supercooling.
   c. condensation.
   d. latent heat.

| Concept Review *continued*

_____ **13.** Precipitation formed in cumulonimbus clouds when convection
currents repeatedly carry raindrops to high levels is
   a. rain.   **c.** snow.
   b. sleet.   **d.** hail.

_____ **14.** The process in which the temperature of an air mass decreases as the
air rises and expands is called
   a. adiabatic cooling.
   b. mixing.
   c. lifting.
   d. advective cooling.

_____ **15.** Fog that results from the nightly cooling of Earth is called
   a. advection fog.
   b. upslope fog.
   c. radiation fog.
   d. steam fog.

_____ **16.** The purpose of cloud seeding is to
   a. predict storms.
   b. induce precipitation.
   c. prevent storms.
   d. prevent condensation.

_____ **17.** A condition in which water is cooled below its freezing point without
going through a change of state is called
   a. sublimation.
   b. condensation.
   c. evaporation.
   d. supercooling.

_____ **18.** In order to find out how intense precipitation will be,
meteorologists use
   a. a rain gauge.
   b. Doppler radar.
   c. cloud seeding.
   d. a psychrometer.

_____ **19.** Large cloud formations associated with storm systems form by
   a. adiabatic cooling.
   b. mixing.
   c. lifting.
   d. advective cooling.

_____ **20.** What forms when the dew point falls below the freezing temperature
of water and water vapor turns directly to ice?
   a. dew   **c.** frozen dew
   b. frost   **d.** sleet

Name _____ Class _____ Date _____

Concept Review

MATCHING

In the space provided, write the letter of the definition that best matches the term or phrase.

_____ 1. hurricane

_____ 2. cold front

_____ 3. station model

_____ 4. midlatitude cyclone

_____ 5. barometer

_____ 6. air mass

_____ 7. thunderstorm

_____ 8. wind vane

_____ 9. radar

_____ 10. stationary front

a. the front edge of a moving mass of cold air that pushes beneath a warmer air mass like a wedge

b. a usually brief, heavy storm that consists of rain, strong winds, lightning, and thunder

c. a system that uses reflected radio waves to determine the velocity and location of objects

d. an instrument used to determine direction of the wind

e. a severe storm that develops over tropical oceans and whose strong winds of more than 120 km/h spiral in toward the intensely low-pressure storm center

f. a large body of air throughout which temperature and moisture content are similar

g. an area of low pressure that is characterized by rotating wind that moves toward the rising air of the central low-pressure region

h. an instrument that measures atmospheric pressure

i. a pattern of meteorological symbols that represents the weather at a particular observing station and that is recorded on a weather map

j. a front of air masses that moves either very slowly or not at all

MULTIPLE CHOICE

In the space provided, write the letter of the answer choice that best completes each statement or best answers each question.

_____ 11. Weather observers and automated systems send data to
  a. the WMO.
  b. collection centers.
  c. the United States.
  d. the United Nations.

_____ 12. Continental polar, maritime polar, continental tropical, and maritime tropical are all examples of
  a. oceans.
  b. air masses.
  c. weather fronts.
  d. temperature zones.

_____ **13.** Meteorologists use symbols and colors to create
   a. weather models..
   b. topographical maps.
   c. weather maps
   d. weather images.

_____ **14.** Continental air masses that affect the weather of North America come
   from Canada and
   a. the U.S. southwest.
   b. Florida.
   c. northern California.
   d. the U.S. midwest.

_____ **15.** A destructive, rotating column of air that has very high wind speeds
   and that may be visible as a funnel-shaped cloud is a(n)
   a. thunderstorm.   **c.** anticyclone.
   b. hurricane.   **d.** tornado.

_____ **16.** An anemometer is an instrument that measures
   a. wind speed.
   b. water temperature.
   c. wind direction.
   d. humidity.

_____ **17.** A package of instruments that is carried aloft by balloons to measure
   upper atmospheric conditions is
   a. radar.
   b. a radiosonde.
   c. a weather balloon.
   d. a weather satellite.

_____ **18.** Meteorologists have tried to control all of the following EXCEPT
   a. lightning.   **c.** tornadoes.
   b. rain.   **d.** hurricanes.

_____ **19.** The front edge of an advancing warm air mass that replaces colder air
   with warmer air is a(n)
   a. warm front.   **c.** cold front.
   b. occluded front.   **d.** stationary front.

_____ **20.** What do meteorologists use to store weather data from around the
   world and to create models to forecast weather?
   a. satellites.
   b. radiosonde.
   c. radar.
   d. supercomputers.

Skills Worksheet

Concept Review

In the space provided, write the letter of the definition that best matches the term or phrase.

_____ **1.** topography

_____ **2.** monsoon

_____ **3.** El Niño

_____ **4.** climate

_____ **5.** microclimate

_____ **6.** specific heat

a. the warm-water phase of the ENSO

b. the average weather conditions in an area over a long period of time; described by temperature and precipitation

c. the amount of energy required to change the temperature of 1 g of a substance by 1°C

d. the surface features of land

e. the climate of a small area

f. seasonal winds that cause both floods and drought

In the space provided, write the letter of the description that best matches the term or phrase.

_____ **7.** ice cores

_____ **8.** fossils

_____ **9.** tree rings

_____ **10.** sea-floor sediment

a. where evidence of past climate is found, high ^{18}O levels in shells of microorganisms indicate cool water, while lower levels indicate warm water

b. where evidence of past climate is found in remains of plants and animals which had adaptations to a particular environment's climate

c. where evidence of past climate is found in concentrations of gases in ice and meltwater

d. where evidence of past climate is seen in their width

In the space provided, write the letter of the answer choice that best completes each statement or best answers each question.

_____ **11.** Two major factors used to describe climate are
    a. temperature and precipitation.
    b. high temperature and low temperature.
    c. season and temperature.
    d. season and precipitation.

_____ **12.** What type of climates are the climates rain forest, desert and savanna?
      a. middle-latitude
      b. polar
      c. arctic
      d. tropical

_____ **13.** City climates are sometimes a few degrees warmer than surrounding rural climates because pavement and buildings
      a. block winds.
      b. absorb and reradiate solar energy.
      c. prevent the movement of clouds and precipitation.
      d. act as solar panels to absorb heat.

_____ **14.** Which of the following is NOT a potential impact of climate change?
      a. global warming   **c.** sea-level change
      b. precipitation change   **d.** Earth's rotation

_____ **15.** Marine west coast, steppe, humid continental, humid tropical, and mediterranean are all examples of
      a. polar climate.   **c.** tropical climate.
      b. tundra climate.   **d.** middle-latitude climate.

_____ **16.** The temperature of the land or ocean affects the temperature of the air above it, which in turn affects the
      a. climate.   **c.** All answers are correct.
      b. precipitation.   **d.** wind patterns.

_____ **17.** Plate tectonics, orbital change, human activity, and volcanic activity all cause changes in
      a. climate.
      b. weather.
      c. the shape of Earth.
      d. the movement of the ocean currents.

_____ **18.** To counter the effects of global warming, humans can do all of the following EXCEPT
      a. recycle.   **c.** reforest.
      b. conserve energy.   **d.** change weather patterns.

_____ **19.** Polar climates include all of the following subclimates EXCEPT
      a. superarctic.   **c.** subarctic.
      b. tundra.   **d.** polar icecap.

_____ **20.** The sun's rays strike Earth at a wide angle year-round
      a. in polar regions.   **c.** at middle latitudes.
      b. at the equator.   **d.** in arctic regions.

Name _____ Class _____ Date _____

Concept Review

In the space provided, write the letter of the definition that best matches the term or phrase.

_____ **1.** refracting telescope

_____ **2.** rotation

_____ **3.** X rays

_____ **4.** solstice

_____ **5.** astronomy

_____ **6.** reflecting telescope

_____ **7.** electromagnetic spectrum

_____ **8.** equinox

_____ **9.** galaxy

_____ **10.** revolution

a. a large collection of stars, dust, and gas held together by gravity

b. the scientific study of the universe

c. the spin of a body on its axis

d. an instrument that uses a curved mirror to gather and focus light from distant objects

e. the moment when the sun appears to cross the celestial equator

f. one complete trip of a body along an orbit

g. all of the wavelengths of electromagnetic radiation

h. an instrument that uses a set of lenses to gather and focus light from distant objects

i. the point at which the sun is as far north or as far south of the equator as possible

j. some invisible wavelengths of the electromagnetic spectrum

In the space provided, write the letter of the answer choice that best completes each statement or best answers each question.

_____ **11.** Which of the following statements is correct?
   a. Astronomers use only visible electromagnetic radiation to study space.
   b. Only invisible electromagnetic radiation is useful in space study.
   c. Both visible and invisible electromagnetic radiation are analyzed to study space.
   d. Neither visible nor invisible electromagnetic radiation is useful for space study.

_____ **12.** Which provides evidence of Earth's rotation?
   a. the shifting of constellations in the sky over several weeks
   b. the period between successive full moons
   c. the change of seasons
   d. Foucault's pendulum

| Concept Review *continued*

_____ **13.** The average distance between Earth and the sun is known as a(n)
  a. light-year.
  b. astronomical unit.
  c. big bang.
  d. aphelion.

_____ **14.** Leap years were established because
  a. a complete rotation of Earth takes more than 24 hours.
  b. a year is 365 days and one revolution takes 365 1/4 days.
  c. a month is 30 or 31 days and a lunar month is only 29.5 days.
  d. the Romans wanted to create a day to honor Julius Caesar.

_____ **15.** The vernal equinox occurs on
  a. March 21 or 22.
  b. June 21 or 22.
  c. September 22 or 23.
  d. December 21 or 22.

_____ **16.** Which is evidence that Earth revolves around the sun?
  a. The path of a pendulum appears to change over time.
  b. Wind belts and ocean currents curve.
  c. We can feel Earth moving.
  d. Constellations appear to change position over several weeks.

_____ **17.** NASA's research on the flow of fluids through rockets led to
  a. improved medical equipment.
  b. automobile navigation systems.
  c. smaller and lighter televisions.
  d. powerful radio telescopes.

_____ **18.** Because of Earth's atmosphere, telescopes for invisible electromagnetic radiation
  a. work best on Earth's surface.
  b. do not work at high elevations.
  c. have been launched into space.
  d. are not effective in studying space.

_____ **19.** How many time zones has Earth's surface has been divided into?
  a. 10
  b. 15
  c. 24
  d. 360

_____ **20.** Daylight time is shorter in the winter than in the summer because of
  a. Earth's elliptical orbit.
  b. Earth's simultaneous rotation and revolution.
  c. Earth's spherical shape.
  d. the tilt of Earth's axis.

Skills Worksheet

Concept Review

In the space provided, write the letter of the description that best matches the term or phrase.

_____ 1. outer planets

_____ 2. Ptolemy

_____ 3. inner planets

_____ 4. planetesimals

_____ 5. nebular hypothesis

_____ 6. Kepler's law of ellipses

_____ 7. Kepler's law of periods

_____ 8. differentiation

_____ 9. Copernicus

_____ 10. Kepler's law of equal areas

a. planets characterized by solid rock with metallic cores, zero to two moons, and impact craters

b. principle stating that each planet orbits the sun in a closed curve whose shape is determined by two foci

c. small bodies from which planets originated in the early stages of development of the solar system

d. astronomer who believed that planets revolve around the sun, but at different speeds and distances from it

e. planets characterized by massive size, relatively low density, thick atmospheres of helium and hydrogen, and rock and metal cores

f. law that the cube of the average distance of a planet from the sun is proportional to the square of its orbital period

g. principle stating that equal areas are covered in equal amounts of time as an object orbits the sun

h. theory that the sun and planets condensed at about the same time out of a rotating cloud of gas and dust

i. astronomer who believed that planets move in epicycles as they move in larger circles around the Earth

j. the process by which Earth formed three distinct layers: a dense core of iron and nickel, a thick layer of iron- and magnesium-rich rock, and a thin crust of silica-rich rock

In the space provided, write the letter of the answer choice that best completes each statement or best answers each question.

_____ 11. Earth's atmosphere formed as volcanic eruptions released nitrogen, water vapor, sulfur dioxide, carbon dioxide, ammonia,
   a. helium, and hydrogen.
   b. methane, and argon.
   c. hydrogen, and methane.
   d. argon, and helium.

Name _____ Class _____ Date _____

_____ **12.** Water vapor in the atmosphere of early Earth cooled and condensed to
form rain, which collected on Earth's surface, creating the first
  a. lakes. **c.** streams.
  b. rivers. **d.** oceans.

_____ **13.** Newton's principle that a moving body will remain in motion and
resist a change in speed or direction until an outside force acts upon
it is called
  a. gravity. **c.** ellipse.
  b. inertia. **d.** resistance.

_____ **14.** The smallest planet in the solar system, characterized by an unusually
elongated orbit and a thin, nitrogen atmosphere, is
  a. Mercury. **c.** Pluto.
  b. Mars. **d.** Neptune.

_____ **15.** Which two planets have massive, ongoing storms called, respectively,
the Great Red Spot and the Great Dark Spot?
  a. Mercury and Pluto
  b. Jupiter and Saturn
  c. Pluto and Saturn
  d. Jupiter and Neptune

_____ **16.** Known for its rings and bands, the least dense planet is
  a. Neptune. **c.** Pluto.
  b. Uranus. **d.** Saturn.

_____ **17.** A gas giant with a distinctive blue-green color indicating the presence
of methane in its helium and hydrogen atmosphere is
  a. Uranus. **c.** Mercury.
  b. Mars. **d.** Jupiter.

_____ **18.** Which of the following make it possible for Earth to support life?
  a. oxygen, land, water
  b. temperature, wind, water
  c. water, temperature, soil
  d. water, oxygen, temperature

_____ **19.** Which inner planets have almost the same size, mass, and density?
  a. Mars and Mercury **c.** Mercury and Venus
  b. Venus and Earth **d.** Earth and Mars

_____ **20.** Which planets show evidence of heavy volcanic activity?
  a. Mars and Venus
  b. Earth and Mars
  c. Venus and Earth
  d. Mars and Mercury

Skills Worksheet

Concept Review

In the space provided, write the letter of the description that best matches the term or phrase.

_____ **1.** asteroid

_____ **2.** eclipse

_____ **3.** *Voyager*

_____ **4.** apogee

_____ **5.** crater

_____ **6.** Saturn's

_____ **7.** crust

_____ **8.** phase

_____ **9.** Neptune's

_____ **10.** comet

a. the point at which a satellite is farthest from Earth

b. the change in the illuminated area of one celestial body as seen from another celestial body

c. a planet that has a small number of clumpy rings

d. spacecraft that first sent images of Io's volcanoes to Earth

e. planet that has many thin complex rings, each with its own orbit

f. surface layer of the moon; about 60 km thick on the near side and up to 100 km thick on the far side

g. a bowl-shaped depression that forms on the surface of an object when a falling body strikes the object's surface

h. a small, rocky object; orbits the sun

i. an event in which the shadow of one celestial body falls on another

j. a small body of rock, ice, and cosmic dust that follows an elliptical orbit around the sun

In the space provided, write the letter of the answer choice that best completes each statement or best answers each question.

_____ **11.** Tides on Earth are caused by
  a. Earth's magnetic force alone.
  b. Earth's inertial force and the moon's gravitational force.
  c. Earth's gravitational force and the moon's inertial force.
  d. the moon's gravitational force alone.

_____ **12.** When a meteor hits Earth, it is called a(n)
  a. asteroid.
  b. meteorite.
  c. comet.
  d. meteoroid.

| Concept Review *continued*

_____ **13.** The idea that the moon's development began when a large object collided with Earth is called the
 a. orbital collision hypothesis.
 b. orbital impact hypothesis.
 c. giant impact hypothesis.
 d. giant collision hypothesis.

_____ **14.** The moon today looks as it did 3 billion years ago because
 a. the moon cooled more than 3 billion years ago.
 b. the moon's surface was molten rock 3 billion years ago.
 c. the moon's mantle was formed over 3 billion years ago.
 d. a crust formed to protect the interior 3 billion years ago.

_____ **15.** Which of the following is characteristic of Phobos and Deimos, Mars's moons?
 a. They are relatively smooth chunks of rock.
 b. They orbit Mars quickly and in opposite directions.
 c. They orbit Mars slowly and in opposite directions.
 d. They were formed fairly recently.

_____ **16.** Which of the following is NOT characteristic of one of the Galilean moons?
 a. Io has active volcanoes.
 b. Ganymede has lava plains.
 c. Europa is covered by an ice sheet.
 d. Callisto is densely cratered.

_____ **17.** The Oort cloud surrounds the solar system and contains
 a. billions of asteroids.
 b. billions of comets.
 c. billions of meteorites.
 d. billions of stars.

_____ **18.** A bright streak of light that results when a meteoroid burns up in Earth's atmosphere is called a
 a. shooting star.
 b. fireball.
 c. meteor.
 d. meteor shower.

_____ **19.** Which of the following is NOT a type of meteorite?
 a. stony
 b. iron
 c. stony-iron
 d. magnetic

_____ **20.** The Kuiper belt is located
 a. between Mercury and Venus.
 b. between Earth and the moon.
 c. between Neptune and Pluto.
 d. beyond Neptune's orbit.

Name _____ Class _____ Date _____

Concept Review

In the space provided, write the letter of the description that best matches the term or phrase.

_____ **1.** corona

_____ **2.** aurora

_____ **3.** photosphere

_____ **4.** sunspot

_____ **5.** coronal mass ejection

_____ **6.** solar flare

_____ **7.** radiative zone

_____ **8.** chromosphere

_____ **9.** convective zone

_____ **10.** prominence

a. a dark, cooler area of the photosphere of the sun, with a strong magnetic field

b. the most violent solar disturbance; an eruption of electrically charged particles

c. the sun's visible surface

d. the region of the sun's interior between the radiative zone and the photosphere

e. a loop of relatively cool incandescent gas that extends above the photosphere

f. the zone of the sun's interior between the core and the convective zone

g. the outermost layer of the sun's atmosphere

h. the thin layer of the sun's gases just above the photosphere

i. colored light caused by the reaction of solar wind particles with Earth's upper atmosphere

j. a part of coronal gas thrown into space from the sun's corona

In the space provided, write the letter of the answer choice that best completes each statement or best answers each question.

_____ **11.** One final product of the sun's energy-producing process is always
     a. a helium nucleus.
     b. an oxygen nucleus.
     c. an iron nucleus.
     d. a carbon nucleus.

_____ **12.** The sun converts matter into energy in its core by
     a. exposing matter to strong magnetic fields.
     b. the fusion of nuclei, which gives off energy.
     c. nuclear fission, which gives off energy.
     d. crushing it with extreme pressure.

_____ **13.** The most common nuclear reaction inside the sun is the
     a. fission of uranium into hydrogen.
     b. fusion of nuclei and electrons.
     c. fission of hydrogen into helium.
     d. fusion of hydrogen nuclei into helium.

_____ **14.** How do the temperatures of the radiative zone and the convection zone compare?
   a. The radiative zone is hotter.
   b. The convection zone is hotter.
   c. The convection zone is cooler.
   d. The radiative zone is cooler.

_____ **15.** Magnetic fields produced in the sun's convection zone
   a. slow convection, increasing transfer of energy from the core.
   b. slow convection, decreasing transfer of energy from the core.
   c. speed convection, decreasing transfer of energy from the core.
   d. speed convection, increasing transfer of energy from the core.

_____ **16.** What is the approximate temperature of the sun's core?
   a. 15,000°C
   b. 200,000,000°C
   c. 15,000,000°C
   d. 20,000,000°C

_____ **17.** What causes magnetic fields on the sun?
   a. coronal mass ejections
   b. Earth's magnetic fields
   c. the movement of gases and the sun's rotation
   d. powerful magnetic poles on the sun

_____ **18.** What causes an aurora?
   a. the visible light given off by the sun
   b. colored lights seen on the sun
   c. interaction between the corona and a sunspot
   d. interaction between the solar wind and Earth's magnetosphere

_____ **19.** The sun is composed mostly of
   a. hydrogen and carbon.
   b. hydrogen and helium.
   c. carbon and helium.
   d. helium and oxygen.

_____ **20.** Where are auroras most commonly seen on Earth?
   a. close to Earth's magnetic poles
   b. close to the equator
   c. only in the Southern Hemisphere
   d. only near the tropics

Skills Worksheet

Concept Review

In the space provided, write the letter of the description that best matches the term or phrase.

_____ **1.** big bang theory

_____ **2.** constellation

_____ **3.** light-year

_____ **4.** spiral galaxy

_____ **5.** absolute magnitude

_____ **6.** irregular galaxy

_____ **7.** elliptical galaxy

_____ **8.** main sequence stage

_____ **9.** apparent magnitude

_____ **10.** quasar

a. star group that can be elongated like a stretched-out football

b. the brightness a star would have at a distance of 32.6 light-years from Earth

c. the time in the life of a star when it generates energy by the fusion of hydrogen into helium in its core

d. an extremely bright area located in the center of some galaxies

e. the distance light travels in a single year

f. star group that has low mass, no particular shape, and is rich in dust and gas

g. the idea that all matter and energy was compressed into a small volume and then exploded billions of years ago

h. a fixed pattern of stars and the region of space around it

i. star group with a nucleus of bright stars and flattened arms that encircle the nucleus

j. the brightness of a star as seen from Earth

In the space provided, write the letter of the answer choice that best completes each statement or best answers each question.

_____ **11.** Which stars have left the main sequence?
   a. nebula, nuclei, plasma
   b. giants, supergiants, white dwarfs
   c. quasars, pulsars, constellations
   d. planets, galaxies, nova

_____ **12.** How far away is the closest galaxy to the Milky Way?
   a. 17,000,000 miles
   b. 5 million light-years
   c. 170,000 light-years
   d. 5 billion kilometers

_____ **13.** Why are scientists able to use spectra to determine the composition of stars?
  a. because all stars have the same composition as Earth
  b. because every chemical element has a characteristic spectrum
  c. because chemical elements do not have characteristic spectra
  d. because colors and lines in the spectrum of stars are all the same

_____ **14.** What did Hubble discover that indicated that the universe is expanding?
  a. Only stars in the main sequence are moving away from Earth.
  b. Galaxies are moving closer to Earth.
  c. Spectras of galaxies were shifted toward the blue end.
  d. Spectras of galaxies were shifted toward the red end.

_____ **15.** What type of star may become a pulsar?
  a. a neutron star
  b. the sun
  c. a white dwarf
  d. a nebula

_____ **16.** What indicates the surface temperature of a star?
  a. the star's mass
  b. the star's age
  c. the star's distance from Earth
  d. the star's color

_____ **17.** What marks the transition of a protostar to a star?
  a. the end of nuclear fusion
  b. the beginning of nuclear fusion
  c. the beginning of nuclear fission
  d. the end of nuclear fission

_____ **18.** Which of these is considered to be evidence of the big bang?
  a. absolute zero
  b. the existence of black dwarf stars
  c. cosmic background radiation
  d. the asteroid belt

_____ **19.** What is a nova?
  a. a main-sequence star
  b. a black hole
  c. a star that suddenly becomes brighter
  d. a nebula

_____ **20.** Why do stars appear to move in the sky?
  a. because of the movement of Earth
  b. because of the big bang
  c. because they are actually moving closer to Earth
  d. because of the movement of the sky